D1622290

# What's the Matter?

### Shirley Duke

Rourke
Educational Media

rourkeeducationalmedia.com

## Before Reading:

### Building Academic Vocabulary and Background Knowledge

Before reading a book, it is important to tap into what your child or students already know about the topic. This will help them develop their vocabulary, increase their reading comprehension, and make connections across the curriculum.

1. *Look at the cover of the book. What will this book be about?*
2. *What do you already know about the topic?*
3. *Let's study the Table of Contents. What will you learn about in the book's chapters?*
4. *What would you like to learn about this topic? Do you think you might learn about it from this book? Why or why not?*
5. *Use a reading journal to write about your knowledge of this topic. Record what you already know about the topic and what you hope to learn about the topic.*
6. *Read the book.*
7. *In your reading journal, record what you learned about the topic and your response to the book.*
8. *After reading the book complete the activities below.*

### Content Area Vocabulary
*Read the list. What do these words mean?*

atomic orbital
boson
distillation
elastic
ion
isotopes
mass
meniscus
periods
plasma
radioactive
subatomic
sublimation
surface tension
viscosity

## After Reading:

### Comprehension and Extension Activity

After reading the book, work on the following questions with your child or students in order to check their level of reading comprehension and content mastery.

1. *What happens when you create a solution?* (Summarize)
2. *Explain how scientists discovered the origins of chemistry.* (Infer)
3. *How did scientists discover that air has weight?* (Asking questions)
4. *How do you use chemistry in your day-to-day activities?* (Text to self connection)
5. *How do scientists build on each other's ideas to formulate new theories?* (Asking questions)

### Extension Activity

Does water hold together or come apart easily? Fill a dropper with water. Then squeeze out some water but don't let the drop come completely out of the dropper. How far can you make the water hang before it separates and drops to the ground?

# Table of Contents

# Defining Matter

Everything in the world is made of matter. Water, oxygen, body cells, and gold are all made of matter. Matter is anything that takes up space and has a certain amount of material in it, called **mass**.

Mass is the basic property of an object. The space it takes up has a number value to show the amount of material it has in it.

The idea of matter has been around for a long time. The ancient Greeks believed that all matter was made of fire, air, water, earth, or some combination of these basic elements. Empedocles first suggested a theory to describe matter.

Empedocles believed that all matter was made of these four elements. The proportion of the elements in each thing accounted for the different kinds of matter. Stone was composed mostly of earth. A rabbit had more fire and water forming it, so it was softer and alive.

Empedocles lived in Sicily between 492 BCE and 432 BCE. He was a Greek philosopher, poet, and politician.

Empedocles
490 – 430 BCE

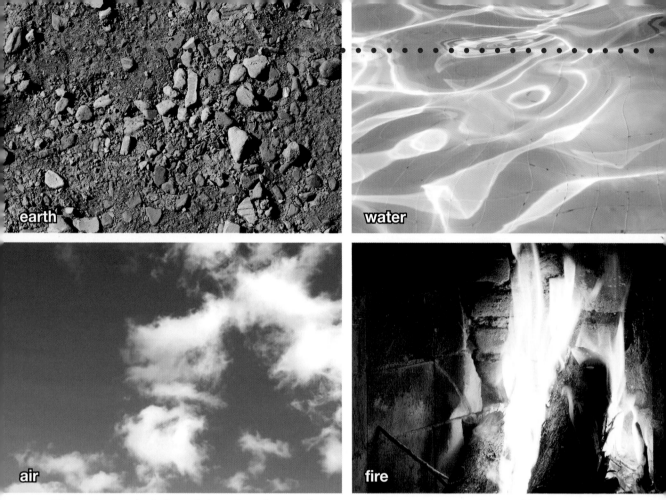

*The early Greeks believed these four forms of matter made everything in the world.*

The ancient Greeks didn't have access to the knowledge people have today. The problem with Empedocles's ideas was after breaking a stone, the pieces never looked like any of the four basic elements. Still, his idea was important to science because he was the first to state that some materials were made of a combination of things called elements.

Later, another Greek, Democritus, proposed a new theory. He reasoned that by cutting stone into smaller and smaller pieces that it would finally produce a tiny piece of matter he called the *atomos*, meaning indivisible. The *atomos* of the stone were formed of the same matter. The stone *atomos* differed from *atomos* of other matter, such as rabbit fur. This theory established the idea that matter was made of different kinds of things.

## Democritus
### 460 – 370 BCE

Democritis thought atoms were different in shape and appearance and that they were all different sizes, with many variations.

**Aristotle**
384 – 322 BCE

embraced Empedocles's theory. He added his own idea that the four main elements could be changed into any of the other. Aristotle held great influence at the time. The ideas of Democritus were ignored for about 2,000 years.

Between the 1600s and 1700s, new theories contributed to the knowledge of matter. In 1643, Evangelista Torricelli, an Italian mathematician, demonstrated that air had weight by developing the barometer, which exerted a force on mercury, a liquid metal.

**Plato**
428/427 – 348/347 BCE

Aristotle and Plato, famous Greek philosophers living at this time, disagreed with the ideas of Democritus. Aristotle

**Evangelista Torricelli**
1608 – 1647

## Lighter than Air

A barometer is an upside-down glass tube standing in mercury. When air pressure pushes down on the surface of the mercury, it makes some of the liquid metal rise up the tube. The more air pressure, the higher the mercury rises.

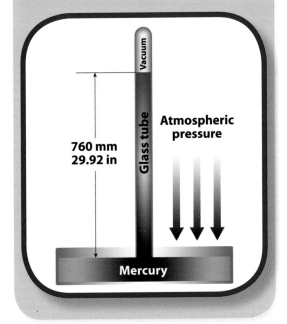

Vacuum

760 mm
29.92 in

Glass tube

Atmospheric pressure

Mercury

In the 1720s, Daniel Bernoulli, a Swiss mathematician, suggested that gases such as those in the air were formed of tiny particles so small they couldn't see or feel them. These particles spread out and were loosely packed in an area of space, moving when people walked through them.

## Joseph Priestley
### 1733 – 1804

Joseph Priestley, a philosopher and chemist, experimented with stones containing mercury. Priestley noticed that heating the stone produced a gas in addition to the mercury. He studied the gas, which at the time he called dephlogisticated air, and concluded that substances combine or break apart to create new, different substances.

**As a Matter of Fact …**

The air around us is made of a mixture of many gases, including nitrogen and oxygen.

*Antoine Lavoisier*
1743 – 1794

The experiments by Priestley, Lavoisier, and other scientists showed some substances combined to form new matter while others broke apart into different materials. Some things could not be broken into anything else.

These men determined the origins of chemistry.

French scientist Antoine Lavoisier carried out experiments with the gas discovered by Priestley. He believed the gas turned certain things acidic. He renamed the gas *oxygen*, from the Greek word meaning *acid maker*. Though his acidic theory wasn't correct, the name remained oxygen.

### As a Matter of Fact ...

Priestley's later tests revealed that another gas reacted with certain metals, releasing a gas that burned easily. He first named this gas phlogiston. He saw water formed by combining phlogiston and oxygen. He renamed phlogiston *hydrogen*, from the Greek word meaning water maker.

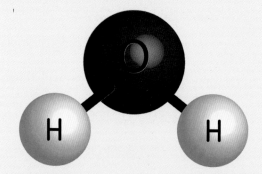

*Due to their chemical properties, two hydrogen atoms combine with one oxygen atom to form the familiar scientific formula for water, $H_2O$.*

# How Much? How Heavy? How Many?

Mass, the amount of material or matter in something, differs from weight. The force of gravity on the mass determines weight. To understand mass, consider astronauts in a rocket in space with no gravity. Their bodies take up space inside the capsule, so they have mass. They are weightless but their mass is the same as it is on Earth, where they have weight, too.

*Weightlessness in space results from the lack of gravity, but the mass of the astronaut does not change.*

**The symbol for mass is m.**

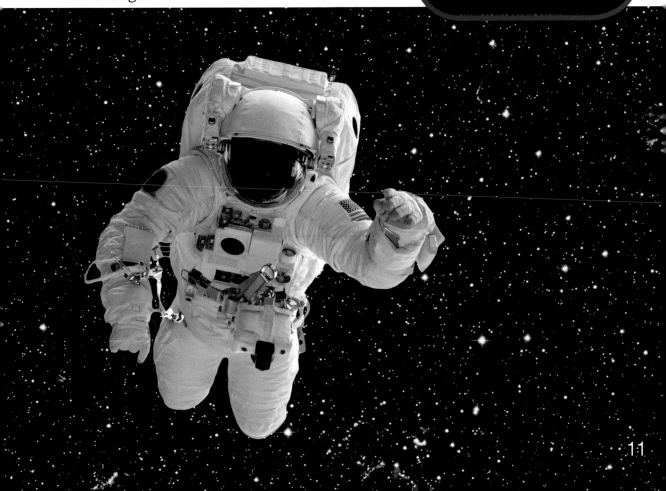

Weight, the force of gravity, is measured in pounds and ounces or kilograms and grams. Weights can change if the gravity is greater or less than that on Earth.

**Weight on Earth**

150 pounds (68 kilograms)

**Weight on Jupiter**

351 pounds (159 kilograms)

**Weight on Pluto**

9 pounds (4 kilograms)

**Weight on Moon**

24.9 pounds (11.3 kilograms)

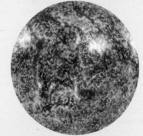

**Weight on Sun**

4,060.8 pounds
(1,842 kilograms)

Volume is how much space something takes up. Solids, liquids, and gases fill an amount of space. That's their volume. Volume is measured in ounces, quarts, and gallons or liters and milliliters.

Density is a measure of how tightly packed matter is in a certain amount of space. Density can be calculated and is the amount of mass divided by its volume. Dense substances have less volume than an equal amount of substances that are not as dense.

*Size doesn't matter with density. The matter in the object and how tightly it's packed together determines the density, not its volume.*

Toss a rock into a pail of water. The rock sinks. If a toy boat the same size as the rock is tossed in the same pail, it will float. Why do some things float and others sink?

Density is the reason. Water has a specific density. So do the rock and toy boat. Rocks are usually quite dense. Their density is greater than the density of water, so they sink. The toy boat is light and filled with air, so the boat's density is less than that of water.

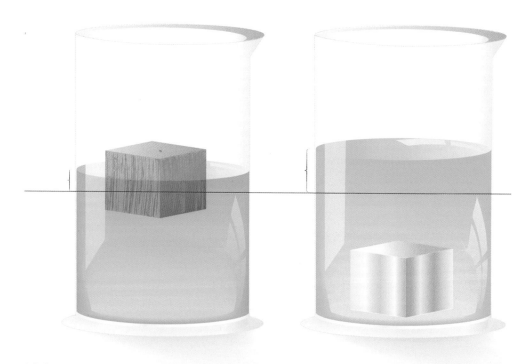

*Although the wood and the metal are exactly the same size, the metal sinks because its density is greater than that of water, while the wood's density is less than the water.*

Antoine Lavoisier burned phosphorus and sulfur, proving these substances reacted with air and formed new materials. The new materials weighed more than the phosphorus or sulfur alone. He concluded that air reacted with the phosphorus and sulfur to form new matter. The weight of the air made the new matter heavier.

Physical qualities of substances are expressed in units based on the meter, kilogram, second, ampere, kelvin, candela, and mole. The prefixes used on these measures involve multiplying or dividing in units based on the power of ten. These units form the International System of Units (SI). SI units are used regularly in science and are based on the metric system.

Much of the world uses the metric system for everyday measuring. The United States uses U.S. Customary Units for its measuring standards.

**The seven SI base units:**
**ampere** (A) - unit of measurement of electric current
**kilogram** (kg) - unit of measurement of mass
**meter** (m) - unit of measurement of length
**second** (s) - unit of measurement of time
**kelvin** (K) - unit of measurement of thermodynamic temperature
**mole** (mol) - unit of measurement of amount of substance
**candela** (cd) - unit of measurement of luminous intensity
http://www.npl.co.uk/reference/measurement-units

## Measuring with Metrics

The metric system is based on using multiples of ten. Prefixes determine how much the base unit is multiplied or divided by ten. Meters measure length, grams measure weight, and liters measure volume. The prefixes kilo-, hecto-, deca-, deci-, centi-, milli- are used with the base units.

## US CUSTOMARY UNITS :

### Time

60 seconds = 1 minute

60 minutes = 1 hour

24 hours = 1 day

7 days = 1 week

12 months = 1 year

52 weeks = 1 year

100 years = 1 century

### Length

12 inches = 1 foot

36 inches = 1 yard

3 feet = 1 yard

5,280 feet = 1 mile

1,760 yards = 1 mile

### Capacity and Weight

2 tablespoons = 1 fluid ounce

8 fluid ounces = 1 cup

2 cups = 1 pint

2 pints = 1 quart

2 quarts = 1/2 gallon

4 quarts = 1 gallon

16 ounces = 1 pound

2,000 pounds = 1 ton

4 cups = 1 quart

16 cups = 1 gallon

8 pints = 1 gallon

# Building Blocks of Matter

An atom is the smallest particle of basic matter. Atoms combine with other atoms to form a molecule. Atoms and molecules are so small they can only be seen with special microscopes.

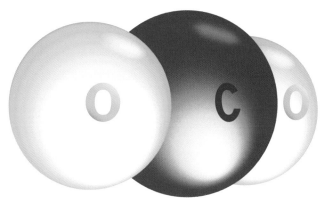

*The combination of one carbon atom, a solid, with two atoms of oxygen gas creates one molecule of the gas carbon dioxide.*

A molecule can be formed with two or more of the same kind of atoms, too. Oxygen normally joins with another oxygen atom to form a molecule of oxygen.

*Oxygen atoms rarely are found alone. Due to their chemical properties, they combine to form a molecule, $O_2$.*

## As a Matter of Fact ...

The scanning tunneling microscope (STM) uses electricity to view and study atoms. A piece of paper's thickness would be made of more than a million atoms.

Molecules can also be a combination of different atoms. Molecules can be as small as two atoms combined, or bonded. They can also be a combination of hundreds of atoms to make a large molecule.

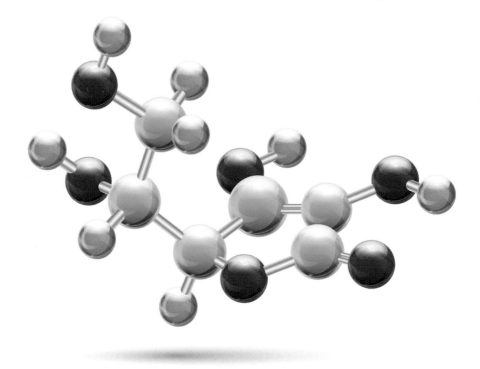

*One molecule of Vitamin C is made of a total of 20 atoms. It contains 6 carbon atoms, 8 hydrogen atoms, and 6 oxygen atoms in the formula $C_6H_8O_6$*

A substance formed of only one kind of atom is an element. An element cannot be broken down into anything but the atoms that form it. Each element has physical and chemical properties. Lead, tin, hydrogen, oxygen, mercury, sulfur, carbon, and phosphorus are elements.

## As a Matter of Fact ...

Diamonds are formed of one element. They are made of large molecules of carbon.

Their structure is different from graphite, another form of carbon with a different structure.

diamond

**The structure of diamond**

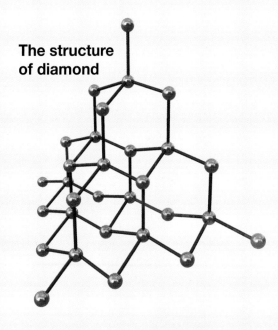

**The structure of graphite**

graphite

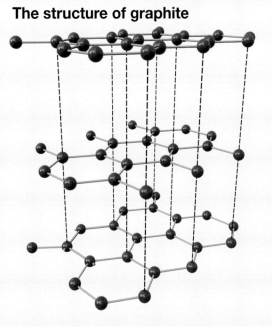

*The way the carbon atoms arrange in the space they occupy determines the way they are expressed. This makes the different forms of carbon.*

19

Combinations of elements in a substance form a compound. Compounds can be broken down into their separate atoms by certain actions or reactions. Examples of compounds include water, sugar, milk, salt, and carbon dioxide.

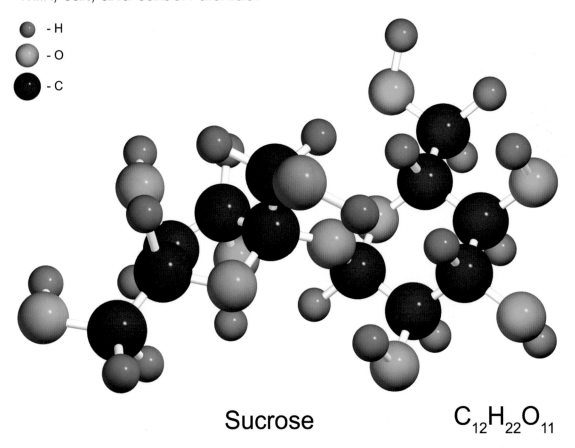

- H
- O
- C

Sucrose      $C_{12}H_{22}O_{11}$

*Sucrose, is formed of 12 atoms of carbon, 22 atoms of hydrogen, and 11 atoms of oxygen ($C_{12}H_{22}O_{11}$). This combination makes a molecule that is an energy supplying nutrient. The diagram shows a single sugar molecule.*

An atom is composed of **subatomic** particles. A large, central nucleus forms the center of an atom. A nucleus holds positively charged protons and neutral particles called neutrons. Most of an atom's mass is in the nucleus.

Many elements have versions of themselves but with different numbers of neutrons. These are called **isotopes**.

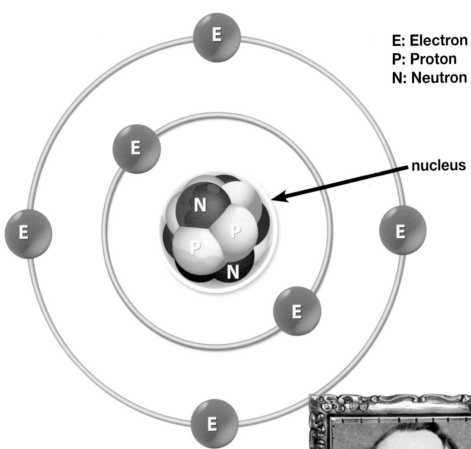

**E: Electron**
**P: Proton**
**N: Neutron**

nucleus

*Atoms are composed of a nucleus of positively charged protons and neutral neutrons with electrons in a cloud around them. Electrons have a negative charge. This model represents a carbon atom.*

### As a Matter of Fact ...

Scientists once thought the subatomic particles were the only parts of an atom. However, more particles have been discovered that make up the subatomic particles. Hundreds of them have been found. These tinier structures are classified by their mass.

*J.J. Thompson*
1856 – 1940

*J.J. Thompson discovered the electron in 1897.*

Rapidly moving electrons orbit about the nucleus. Electrons have a negative charge and contain very little mass. They are spread out from the nucleus. The electrons move in a kind of electron cloud and aren't in one place at any particular time. The cloud size is determined by the speeds and numbers of electrons. An atom that has had some of the electrons removed is an **ion**.

## Electron Removal

By applying enough additional energy or bombarding electrons with another particle, an electron can be removed from an atom. These electrons can make electricity if they are removed.

British chemist John Dalton's study of gases in the 1820s stemmed from his interest in atmospheric pressure. Weather fascinated him. He began to wonder what the invisible gases in the air might be made of. He used Democritus's idea about atoms to answer his question by performing many experiments.

*John Dalton*
**1766 – 1844**

## Dalton's Atomic Theory

1. All matter is made of atoms. Atoms are indivisible and indestructible.
2. All atoms of a given element are identical in mass and properties.
3. Compounds are formed by a combination of two or more different kinds of atoms.
4. A chemical reaction is a rearrangement of atoms in certain proportions.

Modern atomic theory is based on the ideas Dalton proposed. His theory helped describe chemical experiences that had never before been explained. Additional information learned by other scientists modified the theory somewhat, but it remains a foundation for chemistry.

23

# Periodic Table of Elements

The Periodic Table of Elements lists the names and symbols, proton numbers in order, and other properties of the known elements.

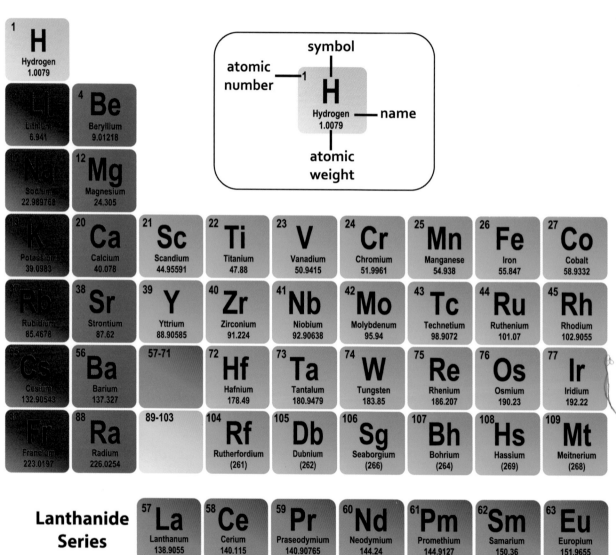

| 1 **H** Hydrogen 1.0079 | | | | | | | | |
|---|---|---|---|---|---|---|---|---|
| **Li** Lithium 6.941 | 4 **Be** Beryllium 9.01218 | | | | | | | |
| **Na** Sodium 22.989768 | 12 **Mg** Magnesium 24.305 | | | | | | | |
| **K** Potassium 39.0983 | 20 **Ca** Calcium 40.078 | 21 **Sc** Scandium 44.95591 | 22 **Ti** Titanium 47.88 | 23 **V** Vanadium 50.9415 | 24 **Cr** Chromium 51.9961 | 25 **Mn** Manganese 54.938 | 26 **Fe** Iron 55.847 | 27 **Co** Cobalt 58.9332 |
| **Rb** Rubidium 85.4678 | 38 **Sr** Strontium 87.62 | 39 **Y** Yttrium 88.90585 | 40 **Zr** Zirconium 91.224 | 41 **Nb** Niobium 92.90638 | 42 **Mo** Molybdenum 95.94 | 43 **Tc** Technetium 98.9072 | 44 **Ru** Ruthenium 101.07 | 45 **Rh** Rhodium 102.9055 |
| **Cs** Cesium 132.90543 | 56 **Ba** Barium 137.327 | 57-71 | 72 **Hf** Hafnium 178.49 | 73 **Ta** Tantalum 180.9479 | 74 **W** Tungsten 183.85 | 75 **Re** Rhenium 186.207 | 76 **Os** Osmium 190.23 | 77 **Ir** Iridium 192.22 |
| **Fr** Francium 223.0197 | 88 **Ra** Radium 226.0254 | 89-103 | 104 **Rf** Rutherfordium (261) | 105 **Db** Dubnium (262) | 106 **Sg** Seaborgium (266) | 107 **Bh** Bohrium (264) | 108 **Hs** Hassium (269) | 109 **Mt** Meitnerium (268) |

**Lanthanide Series**

| 57 **La** Lanthanum 138.9055 | 58 **Ce** Cerium 140.115 | 59 **Pr** Praseodymium 140.90765 | 60 **Nd** Neodymium 144.24 | 61 **Pm** Promethium 144.9127 | 62 **Sm** Samarium 150.36 | 63 **Eu** Europium 151.9655 |
|---|---|---|---|---|---|---|

**Actinide Series**

| 89 **Ac** Actinium 227.0278 | 90 **Th** Thorium 232.0381 | 91 **Pa** Protactinium 231.03588 | 92 **U** Uranium 238.0289 | 93 **Np** Neptunium 237.0482 | 94 **Pu** Plutonium 244.0642 | 95 **Am** Americium 243.0614 |
|---|---|---|---|---|---|---|

 Nonmetals    Alkaline Earth     Semimetals     Halogens     Lanthanides

The number of protons is the atomic number. It also indicates what kind of element it is. Gold's atomic number is 79, which means it has 79 protons. Oxygen's atomic number is eight, since it has eight protons.

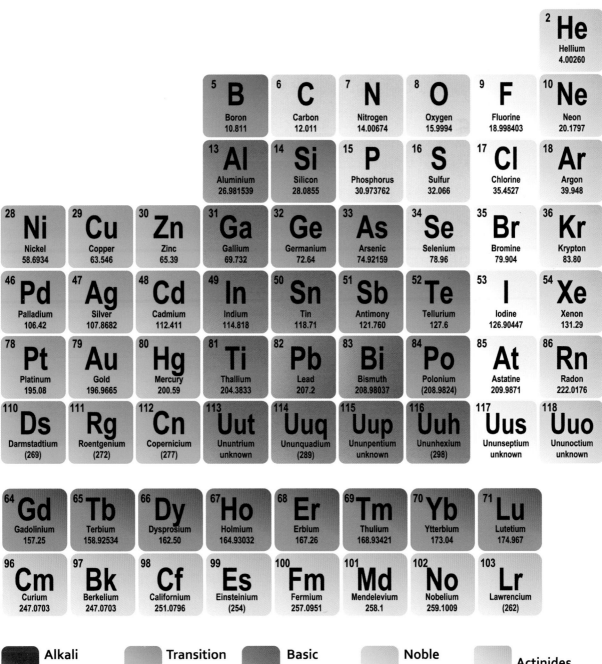

 Alkali Metal

 Transition Metal

 Basic Metal

Noble Gas

Actinides

Adding the number of protons with the number of neutrons forms the atomic mass. The atomic mass of gold is 197 and the atomic mass of oxygen is 16. As the table progresses, the elements are ordered by increasing numbers of protons.

Most elements have versions with different numbers of neutrons, forming isotopes. Carbon, with an atomic number of six, has several isotopes. Most common is carbon-12. It has six protons and six neutrons, making a mass of 12. Carbon-14 has six protons and eight neutrons for a mass of 14.

Dmitri Mendeleev, a Russian chemistry professor, developed this way of classifying the elements, although many scientists contributed to it. He wrote a textbook that became the basis for modern chemical and physical theory.

**Dmitri Mendeleev**
1834 – 1907

### As a Matter of Fact ...

The names of new elements sometimes reflected national pride, such as francium, or the name of the discoverer, such as curium, which was named in honor of scientists Marie and Pierre Curie.

Columns in the table show elements that have the same number of electrons in their outer shells or energy levels. The rows on the table are called **periods**. Elements in a period have the same **atomic orbital**, which is the shells or energy level where the electrons are spinning. Electrons move in any direction but they stay in their orbital. Each of the known seven orbitals is a specific distance from the nucleus. The first orbital is the closest.

## Energetic Atoms

The energy levels surround the nucleus of the atom to form layers where electrons move. Each energy level is a certain distance from the center nucleus. The shells or energy levels are named with a letter.

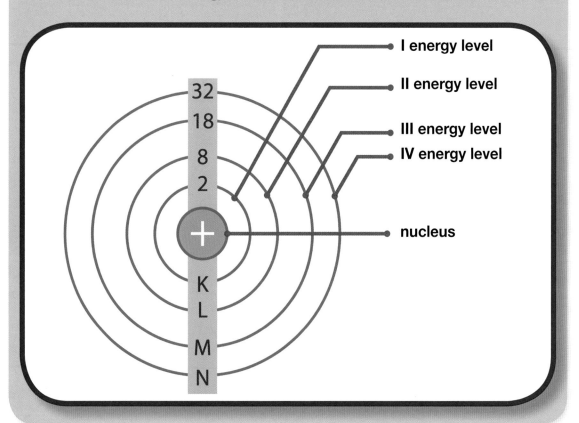

The columns are called groups. Each element in a group has the same number of electrons in the outer orbital. The electrons in the outer orbital allow atoms to combine with other atoms. The first group has one electron in the outer shell. The second group has two electrons in the outer shell. There are patterns the remaining electron shells fill.

Hydrogen is in the first group and has one electron. Helium has a full outer orbital with two electrons and is a noble gas, or one that isn't reactive. The other noble gases are not reactive, either.

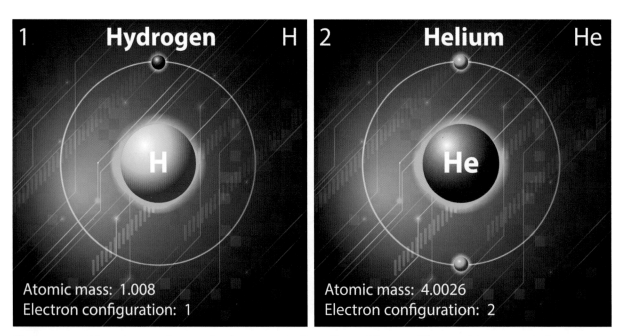

*Hydrogen, with only one electron in the outer shell, will combine readily to add a second electron and fill the shell. When it combines with another atom, it becomes a molecule with new properties.*

## Noble Gases

Noble gases include helium, neon, argon, krypton, xenon, and radon. These elements are extremely nonreactive, or won't easily mix with other elements.

Families of elements are grouped by chemical properties. Element groups are the alkali metals, alkaline earth metals, transition metals, other metals, metalloids, non-metals, halogens, and noble gases. All the elements in each family share certain properties and each family group behaves differently.

For example, halogens are non-metallic elements. The word halogen means salt-former. Compounds with halogens in them are called salts. They are found as solids, liquids, and gases at room temperature. The halogens are iodine, astatine, bromine, fluorine, and chlorine. They all have seven electrons in their outer shell.

## PROPERTIES OF FAMILIES

### Physical Properties
- density
- boiling or melting points
- how good a conductor it is

### Chemical Properties
- valence (meaning the outer energy level)
- how reactive the element is
- does it give off **radioactive** particles?

### Heavy Hitters
Two elements have the highest density: osmium and iridium. Each is twice the weight of lead.

The periodic table has 118 elements at this time. Each element has a symbol of one, two, or three letters. Some of the newer elements made in a lab by scientists are very short-lived. Element symbols are written with a capital letter first. If it has two or three letters, the rest are written in lower case. Oxygen's symbol is O, while helium's symbol is He.

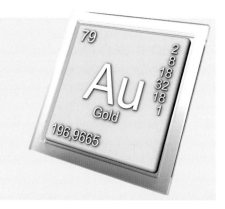

**As a Matter of Fact ...**

Some symbols don't match the names we know them by. Some come from Latin. Gold is Au, which comes from the Latin word aurum. Tin's symbol, Sn, comes from the Latin word stannum.

When compounds form, the combination is written in a symbol, too. Water is one atom of oxygen (O) and two atoms of hydrogen (H). The chemical formula for water is $H_2O$. The combinations of different elements result in all the different kinds of compounds that exist.

More was learned about atoms after Niels Bohr developed his theory of the atom in 1913, when he explained an

*Niels Bohr*
1885 – 1962

atom's structure. His ideas were correct, although they didn't completely explain all atoms. Scientists have since expanded on his ideas.

# States of Matter and Physical Change

Matter is found in one of five states. All matter is found as a solid, liquid, gas, **plasma**, or Bose-Einstein condensate (BEC). The state of matter is due to the motion and physical arrangement of the atoms and molecules. The molecules don't change in any state. Only the state changes, so it's a physical change. The matter's state is also called a phase.

All atoms or molecules are in motion and vibrate. The atoms have an attractive force. Solids contain atoms or molecules with a strong, attractive force. They are held together tightly, staying in one place and vibrating. They form a regular pattern. Solids have a definite shape. Solids include elements such as sulfur, nickel, and tin. Metals and crystals are also solids.

### As a Matter of Fact ...

Matter has its own state at room temperature. Room temperature is the air temperature that has not been heated or cooled by mechanical means.

### Stretching the Truth

Some solids are **elastic**. They can be stretched, or deformed, but then they return to their original shape.

*Silly Putty is a polydimethylsiloxane molecule that resulted from a search for a cheap substitute for rubber during World War II. James Wright added boric acid to silicone oil and came up with a stretchy, bouncy substance.*

Liquids are fluids and take the shape of their container. They have a definite volume. Atoms in liquid move faster, sliding and flowing around the other atoms. There is little space between the atoms. Liquids include water and mercury, a liquid metal.

*Solids have a definite shape because their molecules are packed more tightly and have a stronger attractive force on each other.*

**liquid**

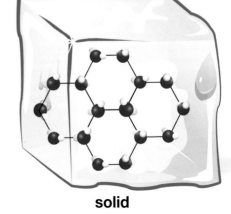

**solid**

A property of liquids is **surface tension**. This force holds the surface of a liquid together. Liquids also have a **viscosity**. Their viscosity indicates how easily they flow. Honey has a high viscosity. Water has a low viscosity.

*The viscosity of honey is greater than that of water due to the property of resistance to flow. Water has less resistance than honey when moving because it has less friction in motion.*

### As a Matter of Fact ...

A bug walking across the top of a pond stays above the water because of surface tension.

## It's Flat. Or Is It?

Liquids have a surface area that is horizontal. The edges, however, curve slightly. This small curve is the **meniscus**. Measures are made by lining up the bottom of the meniscus when measuring to be accurate.

The atoms in gases have a higher level of motion and their atoms spread out. Gases have no specific shape. Gases in a container will spread until they fill it, whatever its size. They flow and slip over and around other atoms and can easily be compressed. Gases include hydrogen, helium, and oxygen.

gas

Plasmas are superheated gas with electrically charged particles. Their electrons are pulled away from the atoms. This causes the gas to have characteristics different than regular gases. Electric and magnetic fields surrounding the Earth and the magnetic fields in space affect the plasma's charges.

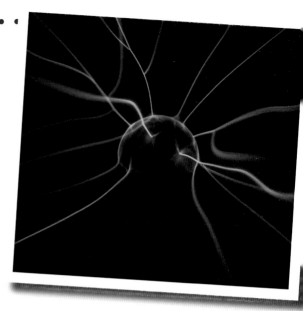

*The word plasma comes from the Greek word that means "that which is diffuse," or partly transparent.*

## As a Matter of Fact ...

The observable universe holds about 99 percent of the matter as plasma. Plasma examples are seen in lightning, the aurora borealis, neon signs, fluorescent lights, welding arcs, stars, and comet tails.

aurora borealis

35

A **boson** is a kind of particle that follows the rules set by Bose-Einstein statistics. These statistics were predicted in the 1920s by Satyendra Bose and later refined by Albert Einstein. They couldn't prove it at the time, other than mathematically, because they didn't have the necessary equipment to show it in a lab.

The statistics predicted the ways particles without mass, huge atoms, and other bosons act. A boson is also known as a force particle. When Bose gas is cooled to the lowest possible temperature, the particles in the gas break down. This is the Bose-Einstein condensate with distinctive properties, such as its particles occupy the same energy level and form a unified whole.

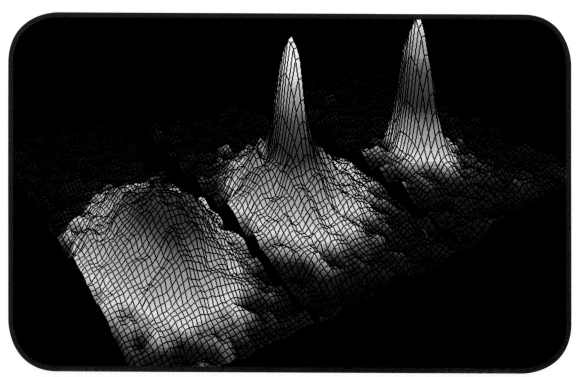

*The three images show how rubidium atoms cooled to near absolute zero behave as they condense. The atoms grow denser and form a Bose-Einstein condensate.*

The states of matter can change. This physical change is a change of state or a phase change. Examples of physical changes include making ice cubes, water evaporating from a pond, and cutting aluminum foil into two pieces. Something must happen for a phase change to occur.

Temperature changes can cause a phase change. Heat may be added or taken away. Melting causes a solid to change to a liquid, like melting a stick of butter. Freezing changes liquids to solids. Ice cubes are frozen water. Boiling changes a liquid to a gas.

Cooling temperatures change a gas to a liquid. Clouds are examples of condensation. Drops collecting on a glass of ice water come from cooled water vapor in the air. Certain solids will evaporate directly from a solid to a gas during **sublimation**. Dry ice disappearing directly into the air is sublimation.

**Changing States**

Gas

Liquid

Evaporation
Condensation

Sublimation
Deposition

Solid

Freezing
Melting

*Deposition happens when a gas changes directly to a solid, like when water vapor turns to frost on a cold morning.*

37

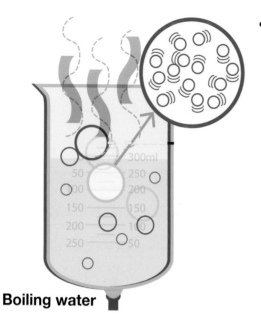
**Boiling water**

Boiling water increases the motion of atoms. The atoms will move around but won't leave the container, while gases spread out and fill the space. Boiling causes the gases to leave the container and move into the surrounding air.

*Reduced air pressure in high elevations allows water and other liquids to boil at a lower temperature.*

Pressure also affects a substance's physical changes. Increasing the pressure raises the boiling point. Food in a pressure cooker will be done faster because of the increased temperature from the pressure.

If you blend two or more substances together, you make a mixture, but the substances don't chemically combine. A mixture can have different amounts of materials each time and can be separated by filtering or distilling. **Distillation** is making a liquid pure by heating it and later cooling it. Ink, metal alloys, and seawater are mixtures.

Solutions are solids, liquids, or gases mixed in liquids. The molecules spread out evenly and remain mixed. The matter doesn't settle out. Solutions can be homogenous, where all the matter is evenly spread apart and mixed. Heterogeneous solutions include a combination of materials that are not all the same.

Sand mixed with water will settle out. It's a mixture. Sugar in water remains mixed. Both of these are mixtures. However, the sugar water is also a solution. As a solution, the sugar will remain mixed and won't settle on the bottom. Mixing substances will allow the properties to remain the same. If they combine into a compound, they will have different properties.

*This heterogeneous mixture consists of water, oil, and sand. The more dense sand has settled out of the mixture and lies on the bottom of the beaker.*

# Chemical Change

Physical changes affect only the phase of the matter. The molecules remain the same in any state. Chemical changes result in a new material or compound that may look nothing at all like the elements that formed it.

A car body rusting is a chemical change. The iron in the metal reacts with the oxygen in the air. Rust is a result of their chemical reaction. Breaking the bonds and creating new ones form iron oxide ($FeO_2$).

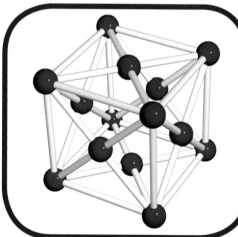

**Iron (Fe) molecule**

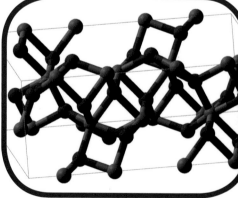

**Iron oxide (FeO2) molecule**

Chemical changes break or create new bonds among atoms. This allows the atoms to combine in different ways to form another kind of compound. All molecules are bonded, which means they react and join together. Bonds are formed in several different ways. Breaking the bonds or making new ones will cause the atoms to rearrange into new matter.

**As a Matter of Fact ...**
Reactions take place with atoms, molecules, compounds, or ions. The reactions of chemical changes can be a single change or a series of reactions.

Electrons orbit in shells. Each shell holds only a certain number of electrons. Shells with a full count of electrons are stable. Shells with fewer electrons than their maximum are less stable. Shells missing only one electron in the outer shell are especially reactive.

**Hydrogen atom**

**Helium atom**

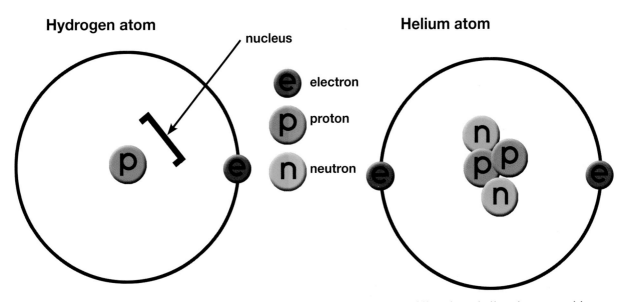

nucleus

electron

proton

neutron

*Hydrogen is unstable and readily combines with other elements to fill its first shell. Helium is stable due to having its outer shell filled.*

All matter is made from the atoms of the elements. They combine in a variety of ways in distinct proportions. Atoms joining may form molecules that contain as few as two atoms up to thousands of combined atoms.

As scientists studied, they began to see a pattern in how molecules combined. The numbers in each element making up a compound stayed the same. They had the same formula. Joseph Proust, a French chemist, proposed in the late 1700s that elements reacted in defined proportions every time they were tested.

Proust's recognition that the patterns repeated when atoms were combined led him to recognize and develop the Law of Definite Proportions. The Law of Definite Proportions shows that when more than the normal proportion of reacting atoms are combined, the extra atoms remain unchanged.

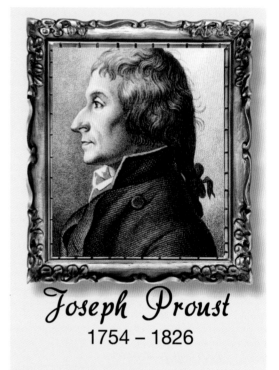

**Joseph Proust**
1754 – 1826

**Wondrous Water**
Proust experimented by combining oxygen with different elements. Two parts of oxygen always combined with one part of hydrogen to make water, or $H_2O$.

The sciences of chemistry and physics look for and identify patterns. From patterns, scientists identify physical laws. They express them in mathematical equations. Among others, Priestley and Lavoisier established the beginnings of chemistry. John Dalton made sense of their information, developing the first modern era atomic theory. Their discoveries led to improvements on their ideas.

As early as the 1660s, Robert Boyle named the element as the basic building blocks of all matter. Today, the atom is understood as a complex system of particles that form all matter.

## Laws Must be Obeyed!

The Law of Conservation of Mass says matter can be changed from one form to another. However, the total amount of mass does not change in physical and chemical reactions. It remains the same. The final materials may appear different, but the amount is constant.

The ashes that remain after burning a log may appear to be less matter than the wood put in. Gases from the burning process can't be seen, but if captured, their mass combined with the ashes will be roughly equal to the log's mass before it was burned.

Robert Boyle
1627 – 1691

## Test Your Family's Baking Soda and Observe a Chemical Reaction

Baking soda is used in baking to make the food lighter. It causes a chemical reaction, giving off carbon dioxide and other products when mixed with an acid. Often, the acid it is mixed with is buttermilk or yogurt.

However, baking soda gets old and loses it reactivity after about 18 months. You can see the reaction when you conduct the following test to see if your baking soda is too old by observing whether it gives off bubbles of carbon dioxide ($CO_2$).

### Materials

- 1 teaspoon (5 ml) baking soda from a box of previously used, open baking soda
- ¼ teaspoon (1 ml) of vinegar
- measuring spoons
- cup or small round container

> The chemical formula for baking soda is $NaHCO_3$. Baking soda is actually the compound sodium bicarbonate, also called sodium hydrogen carbonate. Vinegar's formula is $CH_3COO-NA+$.

### Procedure

1. Measure out one teaspoon (5 ml) of baking soda and put it in the container or cup.
2. Measure out ¼ (1 ml) teaspoon of vinegar.
3. Pour the vinegar into the cup with baking soda.
4. Observe. If the baking soda is reactive, you will see bubbles of carbon dioxide coming out.

### Conclusion

The chemical formula for this compound would be:

$NaHCO_3 + CH_3COOH => CH_3COO-Na+ + H_2O + CO_2$

baking soda + vinegar (yields) sodium acetate plus _____plus _____.

1. Identify the two missing parts of the equation from their chemical formula.

2. Is your baking soda still good? Explain why or why not.

## Activity

### Can You Change a Substance's Density?

When water is frozen, its density is lighter than the liquid form of water. What happens to a floating piece of ice when it melts?

### Materials

- baby oil
- vegetable or corn oil
- cubes of ice
- container of food coloring
- clear glass or jar

### Procedure

1. Put two drops of food coloring into the clear jar or glass.
2. Fill half the jar with corn or vegetable oil.
3. Fill the rest of the jar almost full with baby oil.
4. Carefully set the cube of ice into the jar.
5. Observe the ice cube. It might take some time.
6. Note how it looks while melting.
7. Notice where the drops that melt go.

### Observe and Report

1. What did the ice cube do?
2. Where did the melted drops go?
3. What happened with the food coloring?
4. Which oil is less dense?
5. What did you learn about water melting from the ice?

**Answers**

Baby oil is less dense than corn or vegetable oil. Baby oil floats above the vegetable oil. The ice cubes are frozen water. Frozen water is less dense than ice. The water falls to the bottom and mixes with the food coloring.

## Careers in Chemistry

There are a number of chemistry branches, including organic chemistry, inorganic chemistry, physical chemistry, and materials chemistry. A bachelor's degree is needed for chemistry jobs, as well as a graduate degree to do research. Chemistry majors can work in labs or offices.

# Glossary

**atomic orbital** (uh-TAH-mik OR-bit-uhl): the cloud of electrons spinning in the respective shell or energy level around the nucleus

**boson** (BOH-suhn): kinds of particles that follow the rules of the Bose-Einstein statistics

**distillation** (dis-tuh-LAY-shuhn): purifying a liquid by first heating it and then cooling it

**elastic** (i-LAS-tik): the ability of a solid to be stretched or deformed but return to the original shape

**ion** (EYE-ahn): an atom that has had all the electrons removed

**isotopes** (EYE-suh-tophs): a version of the same element with a different number of neutrons than the original element

**mass** (MAS): the amount of material in a substance

**meniscus** (muh-NIS-kuhs): the small curve in the horizontal line at the top of a liquid in a container

**periods** (PEER-ee-uhds): the rows in the Periodic Table of Elements that show the atomic orbital

**plasma** (PLAZ-muh): a superheated gas with the electrons removed that doesn't behave like a gas

**radioactive** (ray-dee-oh-AK-tiv): materials made up of atoms whose nuclei break down, giving off harmful radiation

**subatomic** (suhb-uh-TAH-mik): the tiny parts that make up atoms, such as protons, neutrons, and electrons

**sublimation** (suhb-lih-MAY-shuhn): a physical change in the state of matter when a solid goes directly to a gas by evaporatation

**surface tension** (SUR-fis TEN-shuhn): a force holding the surface of a liquid together

**viscosity** (viz-KAH-si-tee): how easily a liquid will flow

# Index

# Show What You Know

1. What kind of change would digesting your lunch be considered?
2. What makes the metric system an easier system to use than the U.S. standard measures?
3. Explain how Dalton's atomic theory caused a change in the way people thought about the things that made the world.
4. Explain how the Periodic Table of Elements is organized.
5. Compare and contrast three of the states of matter.

# Websites to Visit

www.idahoptv.org/sciencetrek/topics/matter/facts.cfm

http://science.k12flash.com/statesofmatter.html

www.nyu.edu/pages/mathmol/textbook/whatismatter.html

# About the Author

Shirley Duke has always been interested in science and how the world works. She thinks the Periodic Table of Elements is fun to read and useful in many parts of life. She lives in the Jemez Mountains of New Mexico with her husband.

**Meet The Author!**
www.meetREMauthors.com

PHOTO CREDITS: Cover and title page: background ©Nguyen Kim Thien, atom © baldyrgan; page 4-5 © Albert Pego, page 5 inset http://wellcomeimages.org/indexplus/image/V0001768.html; page 6 © Spectral-Design, bottom photo © wawritto, page 7 © PathDoc; page 8 Plato © Marie-Lan Nguyen, page 9 barometer © Milagli; page 10 Antoine Lavoisier © Georgios Kollidas, molecule © T and Z, page 11 © lculig; page 12 © Jupiter and Earth © MarcelClemens, Pluto © Yury Dmitrienko, moon © godrick, sun © Triff, dog © Susan Schmitz, page 13 wood © Jaroslaw Grudzinski, pebble © NRT; page 14 and 17 © Designua; page 18 © Macrovector, page 19 illustrations © sciencepics, diamond photo © fivespots; page 20 © Vasilyev, page 21 © Designua; page 22 © Roman Sigaev, page 24-25 © okili77, page 27 © yarn; page 28 © BlueRingMedia; page 30 © Ola-ola, page 31 © molekuul.be; page 32 top © SherSor, glass with molecules © Designua, page 33 honey © Olga Miltsova, water © kebabs, bug © optimarc; page 34 top © Andrey_Kuzmin, middle © Designua, bottom © Olena Tur, page 35 top © PNSJ88, bottom © Strahil Dimitrov; page 37 © Designua; page 38 illustration © yarn, photo © Toa55, page 39 © Dotta 2; page 40 photo © IkeHayden, iron molecule © Vasilyev, page 41 © Designua; page 43 © Petekub top, Tami Freed bottom

Edited by: Keli Sipperley

Cover and Interior design by: Nicola Stratford     www.nicolastratford.com

**Library of Congress PCN Data**

What's The Matter? / Shirley Duke
(Let's Explore Science)
ISBN 978-1-68191-393-3 (hard cover)
ISBN 978-1-68191-435-0 (soft cover)
ISBN 978-1-68191-474-9 (e-Book)

Library of Congress Control Number: 2015951560

Printed in the United States of America, North Mankato, Minnesota

**Also Available as:**

**e-Books**
ROURKE'S